PUTTING KIDS FIRST

BY

MICHAEL L. ODDENINO

**FAMILY CONNECTIONS
PUBLISHING**

PUTTING KIDS FIRST

ISBN 1-884862-03-9

Printed in the United States of America

Cover design and illustrations by Jeff Carter

If unavailable in local bookstores, additional copies of this book may be
purchased by writing the publisher at the above address.

This book is dedicated to

Catherine, Daren, Devin and A.J.

my kids, who are continually teaching me how little I know, and how to enjoy the wonder of learning and growing.

ACKNOWLEDGEMENTS

To the many generous contributors in the creation of this book, I am extremely grateful. I enjoyed the privilege of receiving assistance from many kind-hearted people, too numerous to name them all but all are appreciated.

Special gratitude and thanks to

Sterling Myers and *Joann Myers* for reviewing early drafts and offering helpful suggestions.

Anna Keller and *Dan Gold* for making insightful and encouraging comments that allowed an early version to break free of its initial limitations.

Natalie A. Arnett for her helpful last-minute editing contributions.

Jeff Carter for his powerful imagery and positive spirit.

Dr James Papen for all his "suggestions."

Sonny Burmeister for his longstanding support and invaluable research.

Roger Doeren for championing this book and for his research assistance.

Colleen Oddenino for her careful editing and encouragement.

Todd Hester for his creative genius that allowed the book, like the Tin Man, to get a heart.

Elizabeth Hickey for being the indispensable midwife in the birthing process of this book.

CONTENTS

FOREWORD

Since graduating from the University of Virginia School of Law, being married and divorced myself with children, and handling divorces in the 70's, 80's and 90's, I have seen many children of divorce torn apart by warring parents. Parents time and time again make the same mistake of trying to get even with each other while forgetting the devastating effects their behavior has on the children.

I have never seen one child benefit from a vindictive court battle but I have seen many helped by parents who put aside their own desires and work out positive arrangements for the children. Many children could have been saved from ugly, horrible childhood experiences if the parents had been willing to do one simple thing - PUT THE KIDS FIRST. It's a simple mindset that will not only save children from a nightmare of emotional problems but also help the parents to overcome the natural urge to hurt someone who has hurt you. Believe me, litigation is not the solution for children, it is the choice of the uninformed, the uninspired and the unenlightened. Be restrained, be thoughtful and be careful of opening the Pandora's box of litigation. Work things out before they get out of hand. Do it for the kids.

Litigation in the divorce and child custody arena is a disturbing example of how society has chosen to unleash destructive powers upon itself. In the emotionally charged atmosphere of divorce litigation, people vent such powerful negative energy toward one another that it is hard to imagine that those two people were ever able to cooperate in the creative process of producing children.

Are divorce wars unavoidable? Does divorce by definition mean destructive conflict? What are the underlying social issues that contribute to this national problem? What can we do for our children?

The answers to these questions are critical if children of divorcing parents can ever hope to escape the terrible consequences of such conflict. The object of this book is to show that when divorcing parents genuinely seek what is best for the children, negative conflict can be avoided.

It would be unrealistic to say that conflict can be eradicated. Total elimination of conflict in this most complex area of human relations is not a practical goal. It is possible, however, to achieve a more positive resolution of inevitable conflict.

Different methods of dealing with conflict will

produce different results. There are tools the divorced or separated parent can use to achieve a positive resolution of conflict. Tools such as mediation, parenting education, creative dispute resolution and more will significantly diminish the pain of divorce for children. Divorce is an issue that touches the lives of our entire society because ignoring children now is ignoring society's future. Neglected children turn into angry adults who become a burden and drain on society. Eighty-five percent of felonies are committed by individuals who were raised in a single parent or sole custody family. Our crowded prisons are overflowing with adults who were neglected as children.

Tougher laws and mandatory sentencing have not reduced the number of criminals -- taking care of families will. Our children are hurting. Let's change that.

CHAPTER 1

UNDERSTANDING THE COURT SYSTEM

Education will never become as expensive as ignorance.
-- ANON.

Trying to obtain a happy result from the present family court system is like trying to get around Los Angeles using a map of New York City: no matter how hard a person tries to get somewhere, they just don't have the right directions. The present court system as applied to divorce and children is simply the right map for the wrong city. Our courts employ the adversarial system in which two adversaries present evidence such that the truth of a matter will be readily apparent to the judge. This doesn't work to help families in divorce.

The current court system is rooted in the medieval trial-by-combat method of solving disputes. In medieval trial-by-combat the disagreeing parties engaged in a physical fight, often to the death. The winner was presumed to have truth on their side or else the heavens would not allow their victory. As this form of conflict resolution evolved, the disagreeing parties later retained champions to compete for them.

Ann and Frank married nine years ago after a short but passionate courtship. Two children and many arguments later, Ann filed for divorce realizing the marriage was empty and the lines of communication were down. The attorney Ann consulted directed her to compile all the negative information she could on Frank. Ann was worried that Frank would respond in kind and she feared the retaliatory sting of Frank exposing her extramarital affair.

Frank was furious after being served with the divorce papers and hired an attorney with a reputation for being the meanest junk yard dog in town. Frank, incensed that Ann included his marijuana usage from early in their marriage in her papers, described Ann's extramarital affair that she had previously confessed to Frank. Frank's attorney instructed him to detail that the children were in the house when the extramarital affair took place while Frank was out of town on business.

_____

The ultimate evolution of trial-by-combat became the English system of law with lawyers replacing champions to fight client's battles. Little has changed except that now lawyers use evidence and argument rather than actual physical combat to arrive at the truth. Everyone assumes that the system exists because wise people developed it and that its longevity demonstrates its effectiveness. Black robes, high benches and high-priced lawyers intimidate people into believing the system is properly designed to deal with divorce and child custody cases. It wasn't and it doesn't.

Even though the medieval method of trial-by-combat now seems absurd, a distressingly large number of similarities exist with our own current legal system. Unfortunately, the current court system is no more effective at producing positive results than the trial-by-combat method when it comes to deciding what is best for children in a divorce. Indeed, there are those who argue that the trial-by-combat method may be more effective, although this view is generally held by the stronger, more muscular of the two parents.

———————

Ann's attorney hired a child psychologist to interview the children to help combat Frank's petition for custody of the two children. Ann knew Frank was a good father but she could not stand the thought of losing custody to him. Frank and Ann and their attorneys went to court attempting to obtain temporary custody orders while the divorce process wended its way to a conclusion. The court docket was full and the court clerk told them it was unlikely that the court would give them the two days the attorneys wanted for the hearing.

———

The one concept responsible for most of the emotional damage done to the family is the idea that a legal contest must be won or lost. Because of this, divorcing parents are faced with the prospect of either winning or losing their children. The system itself promotes behavior which is counterproductive to the effective resolution of a divorce. The court system acts as a referee rather than as a coach and judges give rulings, not resolutions.

Although a judge's ruling may draw a line in the sand for both parties to follow, that line does not resolve their personal differences. Parents wanting a favorable ruling spend large sums of money on lawyers, child psychologists, private investigators, and accountants in order to insure a win rather than a loss. Children, however, cannot win regardless of which side emerges victorious. This is because children always lose one parent and are scarred by simply witnessing their parents battle.

Using the courts to fashion a custody/visitation arrangement is a wasteful allocation of limited resources. Lawyers charge by the hour while courts make people wait for hours. Crowded court schedules force parties to wait in line for their turn before the judge. Lawyers charge the same for waiting time as they do for arguing time. The waiting time often exceeds the actual court time. The national debt could be greatly reduced by the sum of attorney's fees incurred by parties simply waiting at court. The system simply was not designed for the delicate task of restructuring family relationships in a divorce.

What often happens is that one or both parties simply get worn down, emotionally, financially and mentally by the lengthy litigation process. Divorce and custody litigation is not a game, it is a war. The problem with war is that it diverts energy and resources from other endeavors. The same is true of contested custody litigation. Parents are so consumed trying to gain a decisive victory over each other that they don't properly care for the children's needs.

Sun Tzu, the great Chinese military strategist, offers a valuable insight on war whis can be applied to custody battles as well:

> "In all history, there is no instance of a country having benefitted from prolonged warfare. Only one who knows the disastrous effects of a long war can realize the supreme importance of rapidity in bringing it to a close."

Contested custody battles will, like civil war, decimate all parties. The prize of winning is an illusory one. The cost, even to the winner, is prohibitive. Pyrrhus, the king of ancient Epirus, won a great victory over the Romans at Asculum in the year 279 B.C. However, Pyrrhus is not remembered for his great victory but rather for the devastating losses his army suffered while winning. Pyrrhus' army, though victorious, was unable to gain from the victory because of their huge losses. Two thousand years later, we refer to a Pyrrhic victory as one where the winner experiences such losses that the victory is useless. Winning a custody battle is almost always a Pyrrhic victory. The win over the other parent is too often won at the expense of what is most treasured -- the health and happiness of the children.

The Court set a hearing date three weeks away, and ordered Ann and Frank to cooperate in parenting since neither was willing to move out of the house. Both Frank and Ann hated living together under those circumstances but their lawyers insisted that their client not be the one to leave. Frank and Ann's misery only grew after this initial Court appearance.

Anyone involved in lengthy litigation will get to the point of simply saying "I just want this to be over with." The children always pay an even more exacting price than the adults because they have no control over what happens to them. What can parents do? Truly put kids first.

Kids need parents at peace, not at war. Only by not fighting a custody battle can all parties truly win. As the Chinese general Sun Tzu noted centuries ago. . . "the true object of war is *peace.*" Peace can be achieved without war.

When Ann and Frank received the initial bills from their attorneys they realized they had spent enough to pay for the first year of college for their two children and they haven't even had a court hearing yet. The tears their two children shed each night become unbearable for each of them. Frustrated with the process, the expense and emotional toll, Frank and Ann resolved to continue with the divorce but to use a mediator to help them solve their conflicts. After a few sessions with the mediator, Ann and Frank reached a cooperative agreement.

Understanding that there are many options other than simply fighting it out in court gives parents power. Power to control their own destiny. Litigation over children is not the best way to solve disputes, it is simply the most expensive way.

Parents who are willing to work together for the children, regardless of their personal differences, will help children far more than any lawyer a parent could hire or any judgment a judge might impose. Work together for the benefit of the children rather than using the children for personal benefit.

PUTTING KIDS FIRST MEANS:

▸ Understanding that the court system is not an

effective tool for addressing children's needs or solving a family's disputes.

- Recognizing that fighting to win a custody battle will insure that children lose and that winning a custody battle is almost always a hollow victory.

- Appreciating that children need both parents to cooperate in parenting even though the parents have personal differences.

- Doing what is truly right for the kids by putting their needs first.

JEFF CARTER

CHAPTER 2

BEYOND MEN VS. WOMEN

You get people to do what you want not by bullying them, but by understanding them. -- ANON.

Traditional role stereotypes for thousands of years and in most cultures dictated that women stay home and take care of children while men provide food and money. In the last century these stereotypes have collapsed and transformed into the modern reality of the working woman and nurturing father.

*While attending a men's rights group meeting,
John, whose divorce process had just began, heard
that women always get custody because the Courts are
prejudiced against men. Jennifer, John's wife, heard
from a women's support group that the Court process
was going to leave her financially destitute because
the Courts always favor men on the financial issues.*

*One of the men attending John's meeting
described how the Court gave custody of his three
children to the mother even though she had a history
of abusing the kids because the Court just felt that kids
belonged with their mother. The judge even said,
"I've never seen a calf follow the bull."*

*Jennifer heard from one of the women at her
meeting that she was forced out of the family residence
and given only a few hundred dollars a month while
her husband made over $80,000.00 per year. She
couldn't afford to keep the children with what the
judge ordered for her and she was left with no choice
but to give the kids to her husband because she*

couldn't support them.

Jennifer returned to work after their baby, Mary, was eight weeks old. Because she quit work while she was seven months pregnant, she was out of the work force for four months and employers were reluctant to hire a new mother with an eight week old baby. Jennifer got a part-time job as an elementary school teacher's aide although she wants to go back to school but doesn't know how she can do it while taking care of the baby and paying her bills.

Many fathers complain that the family law courts are prejudiced against men. Men say that they are not treated fairly when it comes to custody decisions. Lawyers tell men they have no chance of winning regardless of what they spend. Men are outraged at what they feel is sexual discrimination at their expense. But men have it backwards. The family law courts are prejudiced against women on custody issues! Against women? How can this be when courts award custody to women in 90% of all cases?

———————

John began to hide money for fear that Jennifer would "take him to the cleaners" as predicted by his first attorney. Jennifer refused to allow John to see Mary arguing that Mary would be too upset under the circumstances. John then refused to give Jennifer any money. Neither Jennifer nor John would budge in their positions.

Jennifer and John were forced to attend a divorce education program. Jennifer learned that a child needs loving affection from both parents. John learned that his desire to provide emotional and physical support for the child meant nothing if the child's other parent is struggling to feed the child. Jennifer and John learned that their mutual hostility was spilling over and having a negative effect on their child. John and Jennifer tentatively agreed to cooperate with each other for the sake of their baby.

John returned to his men's rights meeting and again heard how the Courts rarely give fathers custody, particularly of a young daughter such as his. A lawyer at the meeting acknowledged that it would be unlikely John would get custody. He predicted the fees would be very high. John would definitely not get a money back guarantee, and he must come up with a $5,000.00 retainer for the lawyer. John left the meeting completely discouraged and depressed.

Jennifer talked to her mother about sharing custody with John. Her mother told her that it was ridiculous to think that John would be able to adequately handle the child rearing needs of a young baby girl. Her mother then said, "And what am I supposed to tell my friends when they ask me why you don't have primary custody? Only mothers who are tramps don't get primary custody." Jennifer quickly dropped the idea of sharing custody with John particularly since she was sure she could win in court.

Consider the image that comes to most people's minds when they are told that a *father* was awarded sole custody of four young children. People think that the mother must be a horrible human being. But, people that are told that the *mother* got sole custody of the four children would not think the same negative thoughts about the father. Why is this?

The answer is that prejudice still exists that women were made for getting pregnant, changing diapers and taking care of kids while men were made to do the important work of the world.

For far too long men have been only too happy to relegate all the chores of child-rearing to the women. They let the women get up in the middle of the night, let the women change the dirty diapers, and let the women take the kids to the doctors. The courts mirror this societal prejudice. Angry fathers are usually white males who get their first taste of prejudice against them based on their status alone when they experience a court order regarding custody of their children. Unaccustomed to adverse decisions based on their status they immediately wail at the injustice and clamor for changing the system. They primarily focus on the disadvantage they experienced without seeing the overall picture.

In an attempt to spend more time with the baby, John, who works construction and gets off early in the afternoon, began to drop by the baby's daycare and offer to help at the daycare for no charge in order to be closer to the baby. The daycare center agreed to this arrangement at first. Soon, however, other parents expressed concerns that a young man was working at the daycare center. These complaints forced the center to ask John not to come by anymore.

Men are not fully accepted in the role of parents. A woman who stays at home, often sacrificing her career to do so, is viewed as a dedicated parent. A man who stays home with the children and doesn't have a "real job" is viewed as a lazy bum who is soaking off his wife.

———————

John, dispirited and without enough money to hire a lawyer, told Jennifer to take the baby and give him whatever visitation she would. Jennifer's mother and lawyer argued with Jennifer to give limited time. Although wanting more free time for herself and remembering what she learned at the divorce education programs, Jennifer told John that he could only see the baby every other Saturday for six hours.

———————

The fact that this father was an extremely nurturing and a wonderful parent was not given serious consideration. Until society accepts that parenting is a job that requires both a mother and a father, children will continue to be shortchanged.

The debate as to whether or not mothers should

work is not appropriate anymore because mothers do work and families don't look the way they used to look.

Living with her mother again, Jennifer became increasingly stressed by the pressures of raising a young baby alone. Jennifer's patience with the baby became thinner and thinner. John, although happy to see Mary on Saturdays, agonized over what activities could be done between 10:00 a.m. and 4:00 p.m.

Women will never make true progress in the work force until men assume appropriate responsibilities in the home, particularly in the area of child-rearing. Women must be willing to allow men to learn the art of child-rearing. Many women still jealously guard this area of power in the home and insist that their otherwise competent husbands could not properly handle the important child-rearing responsibilities. Society today does not recognize a man's obligation to provide emotional support to children. Society worries about "deadbeat dads" who don't pay child support but doesn't concern itself with the "deadbeat dads" who don't give time or attention to their kids. A father can pay child support, but spend no time with his children, and still be judged to be a good father.

Today, men are allowed to buy their way out of their parenting responsibility. When interested fathers are prohibited by court order from spending time with the children, society is failing the kids.

———

John's heart was ripped apart on Saturday at 4:00 p.m. when he said goodbye to Mary. John loves his baby with all his heart and the knowledge that he won't be able to see her for two more weeks was almost more than he could bear. As Mary hugged him and said "I love you sooo much daddy, why do you have to leave me now?" John could not hold back the flood of tears.

Parents need to break free of the destructive myth that crushing their spouse in court will prove they are the best parent and that an all-out divorce war benefits the children. The truth is that the only way to benefit the kids is for both parents to capture the spirit of cooperation.

Parents who wish to serve their children well should allow them to love the other parent freely. Doing what's best for children requires the rethinking of ideas that restrict children's access to either parent.

In the business world, time is money; in a child's mind, time is love.

PUTTING KIDS FIRST MEANS:

▸ Understanding that children need maximum parental involvement without regard to role stereotypes.

▸ Appreciating that mothers can have careers and fathers can be nurturing.

▸ Recognizing that children want to be free to love each parent fully.

▸ Respecting your child's right to appreciate the qualities that both parents have to offer.

▸ Creating peace with the other parent while demonstrating to your child your respect for the other parent.

CHAPTER 3

CONNECTEDNESS OF DIVORCED PARENTS

We must all hang together or assuredly we shall all hang separately. -- BENJAMIN FRANKLIN

I always tell clients that when "good things" happen to their ex-spouses, the better off they and their children will be. One common idea in religion and philosophy is that our behavior towards others will eventually come back to us. There is no truer statement for divorced parents than the expression "what goes around comes around." Always treat an ex-spouse the way you want to be treated by them.

Lisa and George divorced one year ago with much bitterness and anger punctuating their divorce proceedings. George is now with a woman and is contemplating marriage. Lisa is actively building her own business as a specialty hat manufacturer. After the divorce George and Lisa let go of their anger with the help of a mediator and began sharing the parenting responsibilities of their daughter Lauren. Soon after George received an inheritance of $40,000.00, Lisa, in critical need of funds to finance her growing business, turned to George as her only possibility for a $30,000.00 loan which she needed to pursue a lucrative contract and save her business.

George at first dismissed the thought of loaning his ex-wife his inheritance money, with which he planned to buy a house. One night when his daughter Lauren was crying unconsolably, George lovingly put her on his lap, gave her a big hug, and asked what was the matter. Lauren, sobbing, told him that she had heard mommy tell someone on the phone that she *might lose everything. George hugged Lauren and promised her everything was going to be OK.*

———————

The way you treat your ex-spouse is equal to the way you are treating your children. Once this is understood, decisions will be governed by a decidedly different and more important set of values. When you look at your ex-spouse try to see the faces of your children. You might act differently toward your former mate. Whatever energy you put out into this world inevitably makes its way back to you in some form or another. It is impossible to treat your ex-spouse positively without such actions benefiting your children and you.

———————

George, touched by Lauren's concern, called Lisa that evening and agreed to make the loan. The loan papers were drawn up quickly and Lisa closed the deal which ultimately turned her company into a very successful and financially rewarding venture. Not only did George get his money back for the loan, Lisa was so grateful that she used some of her profits to set George up in his own photographic studio, a lifelong dream of his. With the profits from their ventures, Lisa and George set up a trust which now has enough funds to insure Lauren's college education at any institution in the country.

It is difficult to think about doing nice things to someone who has caused you such pain and emotional anguish, but forgiveness is the heart of the matter. Get beyond the immediate desire to strike back and understand your actions toward your ex-spouse -- positive or negative -- touch your children in the same manner. Your children deserve to see some positive interaction between the two people they love most in this world. Put your kids first and honor their other parent.

This does not mean that you have to love or even like the other parent. Simply respect their role as a parent to your children. Focus on the dignity of the role the other parent occupies in your children's lives rather than what you don't like about the other person.

An advisor to Abraham Lincoln told him that he was being too nice to his political enemies, that he needed to destroy his enemies, not be nice to them. Abraham Lincoln responded by asking his advisor, "If I turn my enemies into my friends, haven't I destroyed my enemies?" Recognizing the dignity of the role the other parent plays may help you adopt Abraham Lincoln's approach to dealing with the other parent until such a time that a more genuine appreciation develops for your children's other parent.

PUTTING KIDS FIRST MEANS:

▸ Recognizing that treating the other parent in a positive manner will benefit you and your children.

- Attempting to see your children when you deal with your ex-spouse.

- Practicing forgiveness of your ex-spouse to enable your children to witness positive interactions between their parents.

- Honoring your children's other parent.

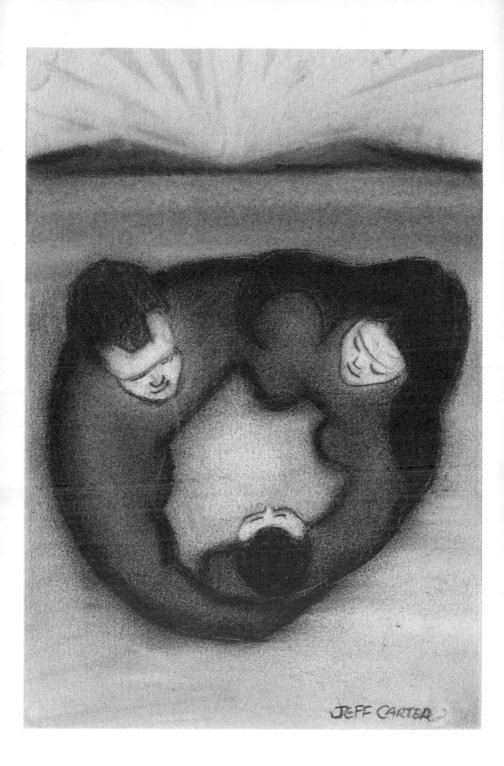

CHAPTER 4

THE BEST PARENT IS BOTH PARENTS

Parenting is the last great preserve of the amateur. --
ALVIN TOFFLER

As soon as the divorce process begins, at the very time when each parent's self-esteem is at its lowest point, the question is always asked, "Who is *the best* parent to raise the children?" It's hard to imagine a more untimely question yet this one raises its ugly head in almost every divorce and is a lit match thrown in a room of volatile gas.

Even though it generates only ill-will, anger and blood-letting, the question continues to be asked, as though it is a necessary element of divorce. This traditional question has worn out its welcome and should be thrown in the same files of antiquity as the polyester leisure suit, the beehive hairdo, and eastern European socialism.

Although Lynn and Roger both graduated from college and enjoyed success in their respective fields as an accountant and engineer, they felt particularly challenged in parenting their two young boys, Garrett and Roger Jr. Lynn and Roger both read books on parenting which had not instilled any self-confidence in either of them. This personal uncertainty caused each to concentrate energies on the boys. Unfortunately, they neglected their own relationship and ignored each other.

The weekly bouquet of yellow roses that Roger

brought her during courtship and early marriage were only a memory. Lynn did not feel any romance in their marriage. Roger felt completely unappreciated and rejected by Lynn's unenthusiastic response to his bedroom advances.   Their favorite restaurants and weekly tennis games were abandoned. Lynn soon filed for divorce.

Roger, although recognizing the emptiness of the marriage, was distraught over the idea of losing his family. He pleaded with Lynn to drop the divorce and go to marriage counseling. He even began buying her roses again. Lynn, already having disengaged herself emotionally from Roger, saw only manipulation and attempted control in his renewed attention to her. She asked Roger to leave the house and proceeded forward with the divorce.

Most child psychologists would agree (a rare feat itself) that each parent contributes in unique ways to the development of the child.   To suggest that each parent can be compared against some standard measurement and have one declared "the best" is laughable. Unfortunately, it is human nature to expect a winner and a loser, and this good guy/bad guy mentality spills over into nearly every aspect of life. Note, for example, the annual clamor for a college football playoff in order to have an undisputed national champion.

Lynn asked for primary custody of the children with Roger having reasonable visitation.   Roger realized that his marriage with Lynn was completely over and was terrified by the thought of losing his relationship with his boys. He hired a female attorney to represent him hoping to offset the perceived custody advantage that Lynn would have as a woman. Roger's access to his children was in jeopardy and he saw Lynn as a threat to all that was important to him. He lay awake at night, his stomach churning, unable to sleep. His work suffered and his supervisor warned him to improve productivity or suffer the consequences. Roger could think of little except how much he loved his boys and what he could do to protect that relationship. In his mind he had no choice but to contest custody with Lynn. He had to win.

This desire for a winner is misplaced in determining the living arrangement for children after a divorce because there is no one best parent in most cases. While there are clear instances where one parent is obviously abusive or fundamentally lacking basic parenting skills, most cases involve two relatively good and loving, though imperfect, parents.

Posing the best parent question sets the stage for an unnecessary and destructive battle. This question is made even more stressful by the fact that at the time of divorce each parent needs love from all available sources and each will seek to preserve the

love of their own children. When faced with the prospect of winner take all, it's no wonder that each parent fights as if for their very life.

Realistically, children will experience both advantages and disadvantages living with one or the other parent. The advantages and disadvantages will almost always differ depending on which parent is being evaluated. Furthermore, there is no question that the needs of children vary dramatically with their age.   The special abilities or shortcomings of each parent may be better suited for children of different ages and having each parent contribute to the children's growing process will only help the child to develop into a well-adjusted adult.

———————

Lynn's attorney prepared to demonstrate that Lynn was the better parent by virtue of the fact that she was the one who had driven the children to their doctor's appointments more often, had breast fed them as babies, stayed off work for six weeks after they were born, and was helping the youngest, Garrett, learn how to swim.

Roger's attorney reasoned that the young boys needed the male influence of their father. He explained that Roger was Roger Jr.'s soccer and baseball coach and that both boys loved going to sporting events with their dad. He argued that Roger was in the delivery room when the boys were born and had been actively involved with them ever since.

Roger and Lynn were each convinced that the boys would be better off with them.

———————

The dynamics of divorce and child rearing defy simple solutions, though society demands easy answers. This attempt to find and impose easy answers on families spells major trouble for everyone. All the money spent on lawyers, judges, clerks, child psychologists and other experts, trying to answer the best parent question is money not spent on the children - the very subject of the battles!

Roger and Lynn each retained a child psychologist. Each psychologist was hired specifically to find reasons to convince a judge to award custody to Roger or Lynn. The family's savings were depleted paying attorney and child psychologist fees. Lynn and Roger each borrowed money from relatives to finance the custody war. Soon, both were deep in debt.

It disturbed both Roger and Lynn to learn that the judge in their case was only recently assigned to the family law bench and had spent his prior judicial career in the criminal courts. Roger and Lynn were both scared. Each worried about coming out of the custody war without a dime to their name. They found their already weak parenting skills falling prey to the pressures of battle. Each yelled at the boys more often, then quickly felt guilty and worried about how their actions would be viewed by the court. Garrett started wetting the bed regularly and Roger Jr. was suspended from school for fighting. His teacher called them both, worried about Roger Jr.'s new behavioral problems.

———————

Children are inevitably caught in the cross-fire of parental custody battles. This is not an indictment of the present judicial system, but rather an indictment of how inadequately the system deals with custody questions.

———————

A mandatory mediation session left Lynn and Roger feeling like very bad parents. They realized that they had become so consumed by anger towards each other that each was essentially conducting a scorched earth policy with their little boys being the true victims.

Experience proves that custody litigation is bad for kids. A better approach is to allocate resources for parents for mediation, counselling and trial-basis arrangements with the goal of structuring a living arrangement that will maximize the advantages of each parent for the children's benefit. Parents can achieve this goal if each will put aside their personal wants in order to truly seek what's best for the children. Divorcing parents tend to disguise their personal wants by saying they only want what's best for the children.

Families in transition need individual attention and care that can't be found in the family law courts. Mediation, counselling, and the ability to have experimental living arrangements with continued counselling and mediation will avert messy custody battles. The judicial system is bogged down with criminal trials and other matters that are deemed more important than family law cases. Family law cases get very little respect and even less allocation of scarce

overworked court system.

———————

Roger and Lynn agreed to see a private mediator together because they could not get another appointment with the court mediator for three weeks.

The mediator helped them explore the underlying reasons for their anger. They discovered that neither really wanted to get married after college; however, the realization that Lynn was pregnant with Roger Jr., coupled with family expectations, cornered them into an uncomfortable marriage.

———————

All my experience in divorce court leads me to the conclusion that finding a good mediator is the first step toward successful resolution of a custody dispute. The critical point is to drop the search for the best parent and instead look for the best arrangement.

Clinical studies have established that no single custody arrangement is always best for children. This includes mother custody, father custody, joint custody, sole custody or any combination thereof. All the studies agree on one point, however: the extent to which the parents cooperate and get along after divorce is the key in determining whether the children will be able to make a healthy adjustment to the transition we call divorce.

———————

The mediator helped Roger and Lynn realize that they were good friends who weren't meant to be married to each other. By rediscovering what they liked about each other in mediation they were able to work together as friends and co-parents while burying the marriage hatchet. Once established in separate residences and not feeling threatened by each other's relationships with their boys, they soon were getting along better than they ever had during their marriage. Because of their changing work schedules Roger and Lynn enjoy an irregular shared custody arrangement

that seems odd to some but works for them. Garrett no longer wets the bed and Roger Jr. has stopped fighting in school.

Many people argue that without voluntary cooperation parents cannot effectively manage shared parenting. This is not true. Voluntary cooperation is preferable but a well structured arrangement, whether mediated or court ordered, will minimize the need for voluntary cooperation on scheduling and other issues. Any type of arrangement, however, will fail the children when they are exposed to parental conflict.

The winner of a custody battle may find some ego satisfaction in the fact that someone has judged them to be the best parent. Unfortunately, such smugness will do little to help the children adjust to the challenges of the new living arrangement. It may be difficult to contain your personal anger toward your ex-spouse but your children's welfare demands it. While no longer marriage partners, you are still parenting partners. Working together to find the optimum arrangement for your unique family in transition will not only benefit your children, it will provide you with personal benefits as well.

Lynn and Roger are now meeting the challenges of parenting by helping each other rather than opposing each other. When Roger Jr., upset with the discipline he received from his mom, told her he wanted to live only at dad's house, Lynn told him to call his father. Roger heard his son's request and immediately told him that dad was supporting mom's discipline and that escaping mom's home was not an option. Lynn felt a great sense of relief knowing that Roger Jr.'s dad would be supporting her rather than taking notes to use in court. Roger Jr.'s behavior is far from perfect but he no longer tries to pit mom against dad.

The daunting task of parenting is not easily handled alone. Ideal parenting is far more complex and challenging than running a corporation or government. Disputes arise about parenting approaches even in intact families so it should come as no surprise when the parents are living apart.

Many divorcing parents dream of the ease and simplicity they would enjoy in their lives if the other parent were to just drop off the face of the earth. While indulging in such harmless fantasies may have some therapeutic value, acting in a way that may let the children know that you are thinking that way will cause heartbreak to your children.

Children shed oceans of tears because of exposure to their parents fighting. Work together, but if you must disagree, don't do it in front of the children. Seek cooperative alternatives rather than seizing hard and fast positions.

Capitalize on your respective strengths. Appreciate that your children can enjoy and benefit from certain attributes of the other parent. Make an effort to agree.

By working out your own arrangement with the other parent, you eliminate the fear of every action potentially being used against you in court. This makes you a better parent.

Unfortunately, there are parents who are "litigation happy" who make it impossible for one parent alone to implement the optimum approach. Try not to be that parent. Children are far happier with two rational parents who are genuinely prepared to suppress their ego needs in order to seek a higher good.

Focus on being a better parent rather than the "best parent." The "best parent" question is the wrong question and it almost always produces the worst result -- a custody battle. Rather than engaging in an unnecessary battle, explore creative alternatives and associate with attorneys and others who are receptive to creative alternatives.

A sample joint custody arrangement is found in the appendix. It is not suggested as a desirable arrangement in all cases, but rather as an example of how the need to cooperate can effectively be controlled by precise language.

There are certainly other areas that can be addressed in a joint custody agreement and the schedules suggested in the sample arrangement are merely that, suggestions. Each family should consider their unique situation and structure an arrangement accordingly.

Also in the appendix is a mediation agreement which is a valuable instrument after you agree upon a parenting schedule. Disputes inevitably arise and this mediation agreement is an excellent method of avoiding costly court hearings while allowing each parent the opportunity to address issues after an arrangement is in effect.

This mediation agreement is designed to keep parents out of court and to minimize attorney's fees. This agreement allows a parent to challenge a mediator's decision in court, but that same parent pays court fees if they lose. This helps eliminate frivolous challenges and more importantly, provides a mechanism for the parents to informally resolve any dispute that might arise.

Consider the wisdom in the old saying, "there is no honor in being superior to another person, the only honor is in being superior to your former self."

Do it for the kids.

PUTTING KIDS FIRST MEANS:

- ▸ Understanding that the best parent is both parents.
- ▸ Appreciating that children experience advantages and disadvantages with each parent.
- ▸ Finding a good mediator to help resolve disputes regarding the children.
- ▸ Understanding that children must be insulated from parental conflict.

CHAPTER 5

POSITIVE APPROACHES, POSITIVE PARENTS, POSITIVE KIDS

Cherishing children is the mark of a civilized society.
-- JOAN GANZ COONEY

Children can derive benefits from divorce when both parents take the right approach. Positive changes stemming from the divorce can make both parents more effective than they were as a married couple. This is not to suggest that parents in happy families should run out and get a divorce in order to improve themselves. This is also not to suggest that divorce makes all people better parents. But it can. Consider local tourist attractions in your area, then ask yourself when you last visited these attractions. The answer for most people is long ago even though many people travel hundreds of miles and spend thousands of dollars to visit them. This doesn't mean the attractions are not important, it simply means that when people know they can enjoy something whenever they want, they don't place a high priority on that item.

Karl, Colleen and kids were the ones that all the neighbors thought of as the ideal family. Karl, an orthopedic surgeon, is charming, athletic and strikingly handsome. Karl loved his five children but the time demands of his work and his drive to be the very best at what he does left little time to interact with Colleen and the kids. Karl's income allowed Colleen to stay home and raise the five talented children, taking them to soccer and baseball games and ballet and karate lessons. Colleen often said that the main requirement for being a parent is to have a valid driver's license. Colleen began volunteering more time and energy to a child abuse prevention charity. Her election as statewide child abuse prevention team chairperson was very satisfying. Colleen was spending a considerable amount of time away from home and with a new friend, the director of a local child abuse agency. He was warm, giving and extremely complimentary to her. Karl and Colleen's children were getting less attention from both parents as each pursued their personal interests.

Karl complained about Colleen's frequent absences and wondered why she needed to get involved in these projects at the expense of their home life. After all, he worked hard so she could stay home. Colleen felt ignored, unappreciated and disrespected for her choice of interests. She felt she was making a positive contribution to society and wished Karl were more supportive. Eventually, their differences led Karl and Colleen to a trial separation, *with each confident that the other would soon realize what they had lost and come running back.*

Colleen got a job as a paid counsellor at her friends child abuse agency. She soon realized she could flourish on her own and filed for divorce. Karl was devastated. He was losing his family, his home, his wife, and his children, all the things which he had taken for granted. Karl was forced to rebuild his life. He realized, only then, that his children were more important to him than his career. Karl became a "born-again" parent.

This phenomenon is often observed with parents. In an intact family situation parents are often more concerned about whom they can get to babysit the kids rather than what they can do with them. Divorce changes this perspective and helps parents appreciate how important their children are to them and gives new impetus to improve parenting skills. These skills may have gone undeveloped but for the

divorce.

Many women complain that fathers who were never particularly involved with children during marriage have become "born-again" parents after the divorce was filed. I have also observed this pattern and find it to be a healthy development for the children. I can understand a mother's concern about dad's motives, when, after years of neglect, dad suddenly wants to be super parent. My advice to such mothers is to let dad flex his new-found parenting muscle. Parenting is the most challenging undertaking on earth and it requires at least two committed adults, whether or not divorced. The more attention the children get from all sources the better. Children receive unique contributions from each parent and neither parent's role can be minimized.

Karl rearranged his priorities. His kids were now his first consideration in all his decisions. The divorce enabled him to realize how little he knew about each of his five children. He now takes them on long weekend trips soaking up all the interaction with his kids that he can. The children, shocked at first by this new burst of parental interest, are now delighted to enjoy so much undivided attention from their dad.

The kids now feel they are special to their father. Karl moved to a home in the same neighborhood as the family residence and the children freely go back and forth between each parent's home. Karl now says that the divorce was a wake-up call to pay attention to his children. He readily admits that he is a much better parent now and much closer to his children since the divorce. He didn't want the divorce but he acknowledges that he wouldn't have made this progress as a parent if he and Colleen were still married.

Even when a court order gives a parent only minimum time with the children, that parent can have a much greater impact on their children's lives than they realize. A parent must not let their focus shift from the children regardless of how much their ex-spouse limits their time with the children. If a parent becomes consumed by the hostile acts of the other parent their children will become secondary. A parent cannot control what their ex-spouse or the court may do, but they can control their reaction to it. Or, as one psychologist counsels, "What you do about what they do is more important than what they do,"and, "You cannot get beyond that which you cannot accept." A parent's impact will transcend the limitations of temporary court orders.

All children will benefit when divorcing parents follow this simple admonition: **DEFINE YOUR PRIMARY OBJECTIVE AS A PARENT.**

Few people engage in business or other ventures without defining their primary objective, yet millions of parents never define a parenting objective beyond fuzzy wishes that their children "be happy," "have a better life than I did," or some other nice generality that provides little or no specific, achievable goals.

From my experience, a parent must have one primary objective, namely:

TO NURTURE A SENSE OF HIGH SELF-ESTEEM IN MY CHILDREN WHILE TEACHING VALUES, CONSEQUENCES AND RESPONSIBILITY.

Such a clearly defined primary objective makes the task of parenting more manageable and, in a divorce setting provides invaluable guidance for a parent's behavior. There are five simple keys for achieving this objective.

KEY NUMBER 1 :

GIVE CHILDREN UNCONDITIONAL LOVE

This means that its alright for children to love, or want to spend time with the other parent. A parent's love must not be dependent on any behavior of the child. Children must understand they are loved "no matter what." Parents too often assume that children know they love them. Don't assume. Tell them. Tell them often.

Parents need to distinguish their disapproval of a child's behavior from their unconditional love for the child as a person. Children need to understand that the parent loves them but doesn't like what they have done. It is very effective for parents to tell children they are surprised that someone as smart as they are, as good as they are, and as wonderful as they are, would behave that way.

Unconditional love provides a solid anchor for the development of high self-esteem. Parents often underestimate a child's thirst for love. Think of how these words of Mother Theresa apply to the children of our country:

"And you will, I'm sure ask me, where is the hunger in our country? Where is that nakedness in our country? Where is that homelessness in our country? Yes! There is hunger! Maybe not the hunger for a piece of bread. But there is a terrible hunger for love! We all experience that in our life. The pain. The loneliness. We must have the courage to recognize it; the poor you may have right in you own family. Find them! Love them! Put your love for them

in the living actions, for in loving them, you are loving God himself! God Bless You!"

A parent can't give a child too much love.

KEY NUMBER 2 :

GIVE CHILDREN LOVING PHYSICAL CONTACT

Hug therapy should not be underestimated. According to psychologists, children need at least fourteen hugs a day for healthy growth. The evidence supporting the tremendous emotional and physical benefits resulting from loving hugs is nothing short of remarkable.

The importance of this key is only underscored when custody periods make contact intermittent.

KEY NUMBER 3 :

GIVE CHILDREN LOVING EYE CONTACT

Parents need to look their children in the eye

when telling them how much they love them and how important they are. Too often eye contact is reserved for disciplinary moments -- "look at me when I'm talking to you!" People instinctively know that if they want to drive a message home to someone, they look them in the eye while speaking. Parents should deliver positive loving messages to their children by looking them in the eye. In his book *How to Really Love Your Child*, Dr. Ross Campbell emphasizes that eye contact is critical in conveying unconditional love.

Again, the importance of this key is only underscored when custody periods make contact intermittent.

KEY NUMBER 4 :

GIVE CHILDREN LOVING EARS

Parents can enhance a child's self-esteem by listening to them. A parent needs to take the time to listen to what a child is saying without assuming they already know what the child is trying to convey. Respect and honor children as people with legitimate concerns and important ideas. Let them direct the discussion. Resist the parental urge to control. Treating children as worthy individuals teaches them, in the most powerful way, that they are valuable. After all, if their all-wise parents listen to them, they must be important.

My four-year old daughter hollered in the car on a recent trip, trying to get someone's attention, "Please, I need listening parents!" Give children listening parents. If a parent can't see their children every day, listening to them is the best way to know them. Writing and receiving letters is also a wonderful experience. Listen to what they write. Explore with them by listening to them.

KEY NUMBER 5 .

DEVELOP SELF-ESTEEM INDEPENDENT OF YOUR CHILDREN

This may well be the most important of the five keys because a person can only love someone to the extent they love themselves. A self-confident parent will not need to compete with an ex-spouse for the children's love in order to create a false sense of self-esteem.

Often parents in a divorce will say they are going to devote their entire lives to their kids. This may not be best for the kids. Kids need parents to serve as role models not servants. A good analogy is the instructions given on airlines. When the flight attendant gives instructions about the emergency oxygen mask, people travelling with small children are told to put their mask on first, *then* assist the children. Is this a selfish approach? Of course not, because if the adult is not in a position to help the children then all are at greater risk. The same applies in parenting after divorce.

As a parent becomes more self-confident in their inherent worth as a human being that will be passed on to the children. Self-worth is contagious. Unnecessary conflict with your ex-spouse can be avoided because the prize of such contests no longer interests you. Parents become free to truly take action which promotes their children's best interests.

If a parent finds themself tempted to engage in conflict behavior with their ex-spouse, they should ask themself if it is going to be harmful to their children's self-esteem and if so, why do it?

An airplane is often blown off course by unexpected weather patterns, but because there is a defined destination, the pilot can make the necessary flight path adjustments and get back on target. Undoubtedly, "unexpected weather patterns" will occur in the parenting journey, particularly in a divorce setting. However, if a parent's primary objective is to nurture a sense of high self-esteem in their children, the necessary adjustments will be made to get back on course. Enjoy the challenge.

PUTTING KIDS FIRST MEANS:

▸ Appreciating that children suffer when you become consumed by the hostile acts of the other parent.

- Understanding that you cannot control what your ex-spouse may do or what the court may do, but you can control your reaction to it.

- Knowing that children benefit from defining your primary objective to nurture a sense of high self-esteem in your children while teaching values, consequences and responsibility.

- Practicing the five keys to positive parenting:
  1. Give your children unconditional love.
  2. Give your children loving physical contact.
  3. Give your children loving eye contact.
  4. Give your children loving ears.
  5. Develop your own sense of self-esteem independent of your children.

JEFF CARTER

CHAPTER 6

THE TEN SUGGESTIONS IN POST DIVORCE PARENTING FOR KEEPING THE KIDS OUT OF THE MIDDLE

Things which matter most must never be at the mercy of things which matter least -- GOETHE

When a young child is wounded or killed in the cross-fire of a gang battle, society is outraged. Media focus attention on the tragedy and police and politicians alike call for immediate action to end the senseless slaughter. Tragically, the cross-fire of parental battles wounds untold numbers of children on a daily basis yet the media is silent and courts and politicians are overwhelmed and incapable of stopping the warfare.

Being caught in the middle of a custody battle is the deadliest danger for children whose parents are divorcing. To watch the two people you love the most, your parents, duel on issues from money, drop-off times, and summer vacation schedules, to simple telephone calls, leaves emotional scars which time may not heal. Parents need to better understand the impact their actions have on kids.

Gary packed his son Tommy's bag, planning for a week's vacation in Arizona. Tommy was very excited about traveling with his dad. The six hour drive looked like a great adventure to him. Tommy's sisters were at camp and he was relishing the opportunity to be alone with dad. As an eleven year old boy he was feeling increasingly strong desires to spend more time with dad. Tommy's mom, Laura, was not particularly excited about this development and was arguing more with Tommy. The trip to Arizona was a last minute opportunity that came about when Gary's friend invited them to go to a dude ranch he was managing. Gary asked Laura if she had a problem with Tommy going with him and she told him she needed to think about it and would call him back.

Tommy was very excited and began packing immediately. The phone rang as Gary and Tommy were preparing to go. Laura curtly advised Gary that Tommy couldn't go on the trip because Gary hadn't given adequate notice under the court order. Gary said too bad, we already made the plans and we are going. Half an hour later two police cars arrived at Gary's house with a copy of the court order in hand. The police advised Gary that they didn't like what Laura was doing but they must enforce the order and they advised him to get the order changed. Tommy was taken away in the squad car crying.

After hearing his mom and dad have a horrific argument the night before, Tommy sat in class wondering what he could have done to stop the yelling. When the teacher called on Tommy he was miles away and didn't have a clue about what the teacher was asking him. The teacher told Tommy he must stay after school to do more work. Tommy became withdrawn and quiet after the police car incident. According to the school psychologist Tommy is feeling alone in a frightening world. School is hard now, he doesn't seem to have any friends and is convinced that he is the cause of his parents arguments. He thinks if he weren't alive then his parents wouldn't fight.

Psychologists now recognize that high conflict between parents spells major problems for the children. Parents caught up in a high conflict situation serve as role models for their children. Conflict is not the sole determining factor in childhood adjustment after divorce but it is a significant one. Kids feel *caught* or *trapped* in the middle of the conflict.

Depression and self-destructive behavior characterize these kids.

Chronically disputing parents focus on their own personal concerns rather than what is truly best for the children. Quite often one parent alone is responsible for instigating most conflicts and causing the other parent to respond in kind. Studies in this area suggest that the three most significant factors in post-divorce adjustment for children are 1) the degree of parental conflict, 2) the degree of legal conflict, and 3) mother hostility toward father. Mother hostility toward father is significant because more mothers have primary custody of children than fathers.

————————

The psychologist sent a report to Tommy's parents. The report emphasized how destructive their fighting was to Tommy. But the fighting continued. Tommy was caught in the middle. If he talked to his mother he heard bad things about his father; if he talked to his father he heard bad things about his mother. Tommy tried to please everyone but the fighting didn't stop.

Two years later Tommy started running with a rough crowd and getting into trouble that worried both his parents. Tommy, however, just enjoyed the feeling of being accepted by this new crowd. A few months ago Tommy was arrested for petty theft with two of the other boys. Gary and Laura realized that they had to take drastic action to help Tommy and agreed to see a counselor. Finally, they agreed to a cease fire and began exploring ways they can support Tommy. They now hope it is not too late for Tommy to benefit from their belated peace treaty.

Dr. James Papen of Rancho Cucamonga, California developed a formula for keeping kids out of the middle. He calls it "The Ten Suggestions."

THE TEN SUGGESTIONS

I. *SORT* your issues from theirs (the kids).

Merging your emotions with the kids is a costly exercise for both parents. Bad spouses are not necessarily bad parents. Parenting is adult business, be adult! Avoid projecting negative attitudes about the other parent on to the children.

II. *PLAN* for the long haul . . . there is no instant soup remedy.

Don't expect a quick fix to a difficult situation. Don't rush your decisions. Alcoholics Anonymous recommends that no major decisions be made in the first year of sobriety. Recognize that there is a similar emotional recovery time for families going through a divorce.

III. *HONOR YOUR KIDS FEELINGS* but don't be swallowed up by them.

Kid's feelings are as real as parents' and warrant parental respect even when parents don't like those feelings, such as the love a child feels to the other parent. On the other hand, recognize that kids rebound better than adults and honoring their feelings doesn't mean becoming a slave to them.

IV. *COPE/GROW* by using available resources.

Divorced parents need one another particularly in difficult times. It's ok to accept support and kindness from others, even if that person is an ex-spouse or former in-law.

V. *MANAGE* the failure, guilt, anger, and blame that often accompany divorce.

Let go of the other person and accept the divorce. You cannot go on if you are tied to the past. Staying together isn't always best for the kids. A hostile environment in an intact family can be far worse than a happier divorced family. There is a real danger in being enslaved by a hostile attachment.

Good self-esteem is essential in good parenting. Divorce is not a sin. Divorce is change. In the case of divorce, change is a necessary part of progress. You must decide whether you will embrace the change positively or just complain that your life is not going the way you thought it would.

VI. *SPEAK KINDLY*, as he who throweth dirt, loseth ground.

It is risky business to get into a mud-slinging contest. Remember, "never wrestle with a hog, because you always come up covered with mud, and besides, the hog kinda likes it."

VII. *HONOR YOUR CHILD'S FATHER OR MOTHER:* they're the only one the child's got.

The value of the other parent to the child is not the same value that you assign to your ex-spouse. The child draws his or her self-image from both parents. Devaluing the other parent is devaluing the child. Focus on the positive traits of the other parent while patiently ignoring the negative.

VIII. *DISTINGUISH CONCERN ISSUES FROM CONTROL ISSUES* for good mental health.

Ask what good you want to accomplish with your child, not what day you want to accomplish it on. Ask what's the worse thing that could happen if you didn't get your way exactly?

IX. *BALANCE KIND AND STRONG* and you will empower yourself.

It takes strength to be kind. There is a big difference between, *giving* and *giving in*. Recognize the difference and act accordingly. Strength involves power under control.

X. (YOU FILL IN THE BLANK).

Ask what you need to do to simplify your life. Since these are the 10 suggestions and not absolutes, you are free to fill in the blank based on what your family's particular needs might be.

"The Ten Suggestions" will undoubtedly aid you in simplifying an otherwise complicated and challenging time. Take the time to consider how the suggestion might apply to your circumstances and meditate on the significance of each suggestion. Take time for your kids.

A valuable resource to help you navigate through these treacherous waters of divorce and separation is the book *Healing Hearts* by Elizabeth Hickey and Elizabeth Dalton. It is a practical guidebook with invaluable insights and useful tools to help you help the children. The authors open their hearts and share their experiences in a way that will help you heal your and the children's emotional wounds.

PUTTING KIDS FIRST MEANS:

▸ Understanding that conflict between parents is the deadliest danger for children caught in the middle of a divorce.

▸ Implementing "The Ten Suggestions."

1. Sort your issues from the kids.
2. Plan for the long haul . . . there is no instant soup remedy.
3. Honor your kids feelings but don't be swallowed up by them.
4. Cope/Grow by using available resources.

5. Manage the failure, guilt, anger and blame that often accompany divorce.

6. Speak kindly, as he who throweth dirt, loseth ground.

7. Honor your child's father or mother: they're the only one your child's got.

8. Distinguish concern issues from control issues for good mental health.

9. Balance kind and strong and you will empower yourself.

10. Fill in the blank for the particular needs of you and your family

CHAPTER 7

WHAT CHILDREN ARE THINKING

There are two lasting gifts we can give our children. One is roots, the other is wings.
-- DR. KATHERINE KERSEY

"When my parents divorced I thought my heart was broken." Sarah, age 9.

Parents in the heat of a divorce often overlook the very real fears and concerns of the children. Psychologists have identified the often unspoken concerns of children going through a divorce and simply being aware of these concerns can assist parents to minimize their children's fears. Obviously, children of different ages have different fears and concerns and what follows is not always applicable to all children. Understanding these general concerns, however, will enable you to better deal with the individual concerns of each child over which you have a stewardship.

During divorce:

1. Children feel a sense of loss, rejection and abandonment.

"I felt that my whole world was falling apart, that I must be a bad person and I was scared that I would be left all alone." Karen, age 10.

2. Children fear both parents will leave them.

"I was worried that I wouldn't be able to see my parents ever again." Jimmy, age 12.

3.   Children blame themselves, feel guilty and personally responsible for the divorce.

"I thought the divorce was my fault because I wasn't obedient." Mindy, age 7.

4.   Children are afraid to talk to either parent for fear of hurting or alienating them.

"I was so nervous that I was going to say something wrong." Ron, age 12.

5.   Children fantasize about their parents getting back together.

"Even after dad remarried, I was sure that my parents would get back together and we would be like old times." Katie, age 10.

6.   Children worry about having to choose between their parents.

"I just wanted to be able to love both my parents." Sean, age 11.

7.   Children worry about whether there will be enough food, clothing and money.

"I was afraid we might starve to death when I heard mom say that dad didn't pay child support." Ricky, age 9.

8.   Children worry about how mom/dad is doing.

"I felt responsible for making my mom happy." Cathy, age 13.

9.   Children fear being taken away by one parent especially if parents are hostile.

"My mom told me that dad might steal me so I was never comfortable when I was visiting with him." Bethany, age 9.

10.   Children worry about mom and dad fighting.

"The worst thing in the whole world was hearing mom and dad yell at each other. I hated it, it made me cry inside." Ryan, age 12.

11.   Children fear offending one parent by doing something with the other parent.

"I always worried about telling mom what things I did with dad. But I knew mom would ask me. It made me not want to do things with dad." Susan, age 11.

12.   Children fear that they are not worthy of love.

"I knew that I must not be loveable or else my dad wouldn't have left me." Rachel, age 10.

Understanding the typical concerns of children enables parents to address those fears and to better provide the emotional support the children need.

Remember, the last thing children need is a battle between the two people they love the most. Oliver Wendell Holmes observed that "What lies behind us and what lies before us are tiny matters compared to what lies within us." Sensitivity to what lies within their children will enable parents to be more sensitive to what they need.

PUTTING KIDS FIRST MEANS:

- ▶ Being sensitive to what children are feeling.
- ▶ Understanding that children react differently to your divorce than you do.
- ▶ Helping children deal with their concerns.

CHAPTER 8

THE BLACK HOLE OF LITIGATION

Where is there any book of law so clear to each man as that written in his heart? -- TOLSTOY

When divorcing parents choose to litigate rather than reach an out-of-court agreement, they give up control of their children. Litigation means turning over complete control to a judge who doesn't know the parents or the children. When parents settle on a mutually agreeable or even mutually disagreeable arrangement, they retain control. A very high percentage of out-of-court agreements reached by parental negotiation and settlement work and last, while a very small percentage of court imposed arrangements work or last. A court-ordered arrangement is most often a ticket to a return court date.

In a situation where one parent is truly unfit, or unreasonable, the courtroom doors may be the only option. If so, make sure to retain a lawyer with experience in custody litigation. Just as no one wants to be the first patient of a brain surgeon, no one should want their case to be the first for an inexperienced lawyer.

Unable to reach an agreement in mediation Nadine and Robert found themselves sitting in the courtroom after six days of custody litigation spread out over three and a half weeks. The courtroom docket forced them to start the trial one day, come back two days later, start again, come back later, until the trial was finally concluded. They were now waiting for the judge to announce his decision. The judge sat in his chambers digesting the evidence presented regarding the custody of their two children, Natalie and Justin. When the bailiff announced that the judge was coming out both Nadine's and Robert's stomachs turned more violently than they already had.

Nadine initially felt that she would have no problem winning custody since she was the mother. As the trial progressed her confidence slowly disintegrated and her fears began to run rampant. It was painfully obvious to Nadine that her lawyer was no match for Robert's. In the middle of the trial she wondered if there was some way to stop the trial and simply start over with a new attorney. Her lawyer didn't seem to know what to do, while Robert's lawyer aggressively pushed his client's case forward. When Nadine tried to tell her lawyer something during the trial he simply held up his hand as if he was too busy to listen to her. She saw misleading testimony after misleading testimony go unchallenged and unquestioned by her attorney. She began to wonder who he was working for.

When any lawyer is hired, they are essentially an employee engaged to perform a specific task. Interview a number of lawyers and always get references. Find out from lawyers who work in other areas of law who they would hire to represent them if they were going through a divorce. Visit the court where your case will be heard and ask about the family law attorneys that practice there. Don't be bashful about asking lawyers what kind of custody litigation experience they have. As the employer, you are entitled to that information before you spend your money. Insist on a written retainer agreement that spells out the terms of the lawyer's employment for you.

The lawyer should be aware of psychologists who are experienced in conducting child custody evaluations. It is vital to have a psychologist involved who has experience testifying in the courtroom. The psychologist must be skilled both in terms of the professional expertise they bring to bear on the family situation and in speaking and thinking under the fire of hostile cross-examination.

The most critical aspect of custody litigation is the attorney you hire. If an attorney is chosen well, the litigation will be contested on a more level playing field. Failure to take the time and effort required to find an experienced and skilled custody attorney will result in a huge courtroom disadvantage. Should an attorney prove inadequate the best course is to fire him or her and hire another. This may sound harsh, but remember, you're dealing with your children's future. Don't be shy.

Nadine's anxiety grew as she awaited the judge's decision. She could not believe that her superiority as the best parent was not properly conveyed to the court. Now she faced the very real prospect of losing custody. It was the worst time of her life. She was furious that her attorney failed to prepare, apparently relying on her motherhood to cinch the victory. Nadine feared what the judge would

do.   Nadine never wanted to see her lawyer again.
She wanted to wipe Robert off the face of the earth.
Everyone seemed to be against her.

A good case requires proper preparation in advance of any hearing.   If all efforts to mediate or settle the case have been thwarted, then you must prepare to litigate. Prepare to prevail on the important issues that will be presented to the court. The will to prevail is meaningless without the will to prepare. Proper litigation involves monumental work by the client and attorney working together.   Establish a specific theme for the litigation and gather evidence to support that theme.

Robert sat   not far from Nadine, equally concerned about what the judge might do to him.

Unlike Nadine, he was pleased with his attorney's performance but he knew that the odds were against him. His attorney advised him that without a particular problem to allege against Nadine, the court's natural prejudice would be to favor the mother. Also, his attorney advised him that since his income was double Nadine's income he could expect to pay a substantial amount of child support if Nadine prevailed. Robert could not believe that even though he paid thousands of dollars to his attorney, he still might be reduced to being a weekend visitor with his children, have to pay a portion of Nadine's attorney's fees, and see money deducted from his paycheck every month. Robert wondered if the judge had any idea of how much was at stake for him.

MONEY

The most common sticking point that forces matters to be litigated is money, whether it be child support, spousal support, or attorney's fees. The money issue demands meticulous attention to detail or a family's financial future could be put in serious jeopardy.

A friend of mine once said that there are only two "rules" about money: More is better than less, and sooner is better than later. These two rules demonstrate a one-sided approach that will tear children apart when both parents only think about getting money. This attitude does not generate the type of cooperative spirit that divorced parents need to deal with the various emotional needs of their children while meeting the economic challenges of their new family arrangement.

CHILD SUPPORT

The amount of child support awarded by the court is essentially set by state legislature mandatory guidelines. The courts generally have very little flexibility in fixing a child support amount. The two primary factors in determining child support are the income of each parent, and the time children spend with each parent.

Under certain circumstances the court may consider unusual expenses in fixing a child support amount but most parents, whether on the receiving end or the paying end, are surprised to learn that the court pays very little attention to their expenses.

The child support guidelines are the result of certain federal mandates regarding child support and courts generally are not allowed to deviate much from the guideline amount except under rare circumstances. However, both divorcing parents MAY AGREE to an amount different than what is dictated by the guidelines. Only the court must follow the guidelines.

The paying parent or the receiving parent may have good reasons to agree to an amount higher or lower than the guideline amount. The guideline amount can be very high in certain circumstances and a receiving parent may greatly improve the relationship with the other parent by agreeing to an amount less than what the guideline dictates. If a receiving parent feels that the needs of the children will be met with an amount less than the guideline figure, then accepting a lesser amount may lead to a quicker settlement on custody, visitation or other issues.

If the guideline amount is low but the paying parent has other resources that would make a higher amount possible, agreeing to the higher amount may well solve other conflicts. Often what a party is arguing about does not reflect their true concern. By eliminating the financial concern, other concerns may magically disappear.

Money is almost always a major concern of the parents going through a divorce. Sometimes there just isn't enough to go around. Sometimes when one household becomes two households the money will not stretch to allow everyone to maintain the same lifestyle. This must be recognized. If both parents can appreciate that financial life is going to be tougher not easier, then, the parents are more likely to be able to reach an agreement that is fair to everyone, especially the children.

For example, it does not do the children any good if the custodial parent insists on the highest child support award possible where such an award will leave the other parent without sufficient funds to do any activities with the children when they do have them. Likewise, if the custodial parent does not have sufficient funds to feed, shelter and clothe the children, it is the children who will suffer.

If either parent seeks custody or custodial time

with the idea of gaining a personal financial advantage, the children will suffer. Many times custodial parents resist giving more time to the other parent because it would result in a lower child support award. This is not putting the children first, and there are many ways the children suffer when this happens. I have seen non-custodial parents seek more time or custody because it would be easier on them financially. Again, this is not putting the children first.

The child support issue can ruin a potentially favorable shared parenting arrangement for the children. Too often each parent positions themselves to maximize their financial position rather than insuring that the kids get two actively involved parents. Each parent must examine their own motives and then make the difficult decision of doing what is genuinely best for the kids even if it costs them more money. More often than not, such a decision will end up saving both parents a lot of money -- money not spent on lawyers -- and go a long way toward insuring that the children get what they need most, two parents who are genuinely dedicated to their kids, no matter what the cost may be.

Child support is clearly an important part of any case involving children. Be fair and put the children first in determining both the custody arrangements as well as the child support. When both parents are truly looking out for the children, a child support agreement is easily reached. If even one parent is being unreasonable, litigation costs are increased and this is not best for the children. Thorough preparation will help protect you from the consequences of the other party's unreasonableness. An eye toward what is truly best for your children will go a long way toward promoting reasonableness on each side.

The judge finally entered the courtroom. The bailiff announced that the court was now in session and directed the parties to remain seated. The judge spoke. "Back on the record. After all the time we have spent on this case let me tell you that I find this case to be a real tragedy. Not because Natalie and Justin don't have a good future, they are obviously bright and gifted children who seem to be doing well in spite of their parents. The tragedy is that you two so-called adults would come in to this courtroom and spend ungodly sums of your own money, money that will never help Natalie and Justin, to publicly attack the other parent about stupid things like what time one of you puts the kids to bed and who makes them floss and who doesn't.

Although we have already spent too much time and money on this case, my decision is going to cause you to spend some more. My decision is that I'm not going to make a decision today. That's right. I am so irritated that you two would waste my time and the taxpayer's money with the kind of foolishness you made me sit through that I'm going to make you do some more work. You both must go back to mediation for another attempt at settling this case. This appointment must be completed in two weeks. Then you come back to me. If you don't have an agreement then you can bet that I will make an order that I can guarantee neither one of you is going to like. Don't try to read into that statement what I might do, because you can be sure that you haven't thought of it.

If you two want to spend your children's future on these fine lawyers then I will give you the opportunity to do so. If you want to give up control of your children and trust their future to some guy who makes his living wearing a black dress, then so be it. You two are good parents and you both better start focusing on your kids because you don't have any guarantee that I know what I'm doing when it comes to planning your kids future based on what I've heard about you. But if you would rather have me do it, I guess that really says something about how you feel about your kids. My clerk will give you a date. We're adjourned."

Many a child's college education fund has been spent on attorney's fees for child custody and divorce battles. Most states will allow the court to order the higher income parent to pay some or all of the lower income parent's attorney's fees. Even if you are the low income parent and expect an award of attorney's fees, you should remember that any money paid to the attorneys, even if paid by your ex-spouse, is money not spent on your children.

All money issues are difficult and no simple answers can be automatically applied in all cases. You must decide how the rules of money apply to your case and how to maximize the limited family resources for the children's sake.

Litigation over children is extremely inefficient, does not produce optimum results, and should be the last possible option for any caring parent.

PUTTING KIDS FIRST MEANS:

▸ Appreciating that reaching an agreement keeps you in control of your family while litigating gives control to the judge.

▸ Understanding that hiring an effective lawyer and preparation are the critical components to litigating for your children.

▸ Not allowing money concerns to cloud one's

judgment on what's best for the children.

▶ Fighting to protect your children not fighting over your children.

CHAPTER 9

SHAPING THE FUTURE

The significant problems we face cannot be solved at the same level of thinking we were at when we created them. -- ALBERT EINSTEIN.

There is no antidote to the pain of divorce just better ways of dealing with that pain. Accept the fact that the whole process is painful and take positive action to deal with the pain. Children deserve nothing less. Assisting the children through a painful process strengthens the parent's bond with them. Adding to the pain your children feel weakens that bond. A parent needs to grow with their kids and help each one deal with the changes positively.

New approaches are critical to improving the lives for our children. Learn from the story of the woman who, while delayed at work, asked her husband to put the ham in the oven. When she arrived home she asked if her husband had cut the end of the ham off before putting it in the oven. The husband responded that he had not and asked why was it necessary to cut the end of the ham?

His wife responded that she wasn't sure why but that her mother taught her that way of cooking a ham. Husband suggested that they call her mother to determine why it was necessary to cut the end of the ham before placing it in the oven. The wife's mother answered that she didn't know but she had been taught that way by her mother. The husband then suggested that they ask grandma. They called and grandma explained that her oven was so small she couldn't fit the whole ham in the oven without first cutting off the end.

Today many things are done simply because

they have been done that way in the past. Present circumstances often require new approaches, yet people allow themselves to be shackled by the past. Progress demands progressive thinking and new ideas.

David and Susan mutually agreed that even though they hate to think of themselves as failures, they hate even more living in a marriage that is generating only negative energy and causing them to be ineffective parents. Each consults a lawyer about divorce and are given the same advice.

They are told they must first attend mandatory parenting education classes before they can get a custody order from court. Even if they agree on a custody schedule they must still attend these classes before a judge will sign an order. A parent cannot get an order from the Family Court for custody or access without a certificate of completion from the parenting education classes. They each learn that the divorce process is quite different since the new legislation went into effect. There are many new steps and resources available to them.

Susan and David learn that after the mandatory parenting education classes they must then participate in mandatory mediation, one mediator for their financial issues and a separate mediator for their custody issues. They learn that family counselors are available to discuss issues with each parent individually or jointly. They learn that if they still can't resolve any dispute regarding the children they each must prepare and submit a detailed plan to the court listing the reasons their plan is one that truly takes the particular needs of their children into account. They learn that it isn't done the way it used to be done.

In almost every case I've seen, one parent would never accept the custody arrangement proposal they offer the other parent. I believe a better way of forcing parents to make equitable custody proposals

would be to use something similar to the major league baseball arbitration system.

In salary disputes the player and the team each submit a proposal to the arbitrator detailing reasons why their proposal is the appropriate one. The arbitrator must choose one proposal. This approach encourages both sides to be more reasonable in their proposal because an obviously unreasonable one will be rejected in favor of the other side's more reasonable plan.

If each parent were required to submit a custody proposal, with the knowledge that a judge or arbitrator had to choose one of the party's proposals based on which proposal was deemed in the overall best interests of the children, such proposals would be radically different from what we generally see today.

Certain factors could guide the judge or arbitrator in choosing between the two proposals. While "best interests of the children" is so vague as to provide little practical guidance, objective factors can be utilized. For example, the primary factor (assuming two basically fit parents) would be *the willingness of each parent to promote a healthy relationship with the children and the other parent.*

Other objective factors in determining the pros and cons of a particular living arrangement proposal, in no particular order, could include the following regarding the respective homes:

1. Form of discipline.

2. Residential stability.

3. Educational assistance for the children.

4. Lifestyles/Values.

5. History of substance abuse.

6. Relationships of children with stepparent or significant other.

7. Psychological evaluations.

8.   Particular needs of the children.

9.   Geographic considerations.

10.   Job stability of parents.

11.   Preferences of children.

Each parent, with or without the assistance of an attorney, would be able to promote the benefits of their proposal while discussing concerns regarding the other proposal. With each parent knowing that the judge or arbitrator would select one proposal intact, each has significant motivation to focus on the positive of their plan rather than the negative of the other.

With the primary factor being the willingness of a parent to promote a healthy relationship with the other parent, each proposal is more likely to focus on the positive cooperative aspects of post-divorce parenting rather than the mud-slinging characteristic of today's custody litigation. Concerns about the other plan could be addressed with the understanding that regardless of the judge's choice, the parents will be long-term parenting partners and alienating such a partner is not in the best interests of the children.

———

David and Susan also learn that the Family Court judges receive extensive training in childhood development and family systems dynamics. Each attorney explains that the Family Court judges receive what is essentially a post-graduate degree in post-divorce childhood issues with significant emphasis in family systems theory. Judges actively seek out the Family Court assignment because of the additional educational training that goes with the assignment. David and Susan learn that these judges want to deal with children's and family issues and truly understand how important these issues are not only to the families involved but to our entire society. These judges want to have a positive impact on society.

———

A safety valve for the children would be that the judge or arbitrator could determine that neither proposal is sufficiently reasonable and send both parties back to the drawing board. The judge would have much more freedom to openly discuss what the judge feels is wrong and what the parties need to do before they resubmit their proposals. This is not intended to provide a detailed mechanism for solving all possible disputes, rather, a framework in which parents can work positively to resolve conflict.

As parents become less focused on their "rights" and more focused on long term family solutions, children will reap rich dividends. Parents concentrating on "rights" are often like an automobile approaching an intersection. While the light may indicate green, giving you the legal "right" to proceed through the intersection, if you see an eighteen-wheeler rumbling toward the intersection at eighty miles an hour with no time to stop for the red light you may want to defer your legal "right" to proceed. Insist on exercising your "right" and you may be "dead right."

We cannot assume that we know so much about our children or what's best for them that we disregard new and creative approaches. As Daniel Boorstin, former librarian of the Library of Congress, said, "The main obstacle to progress is not ignorance, but the illusion of knowledge."

PUTTING KIDS FIRST MEANS:

► Taking action to deal with the pain of divorce rather than fighting the pain.

► Improving our approaches to divorce to enable children to flourish.

► Seeking equitable custody arrangements based on objective factors related to the children's well-being.

► Going beyond the illusion of knowledge to embrace progressive approaches for the children.

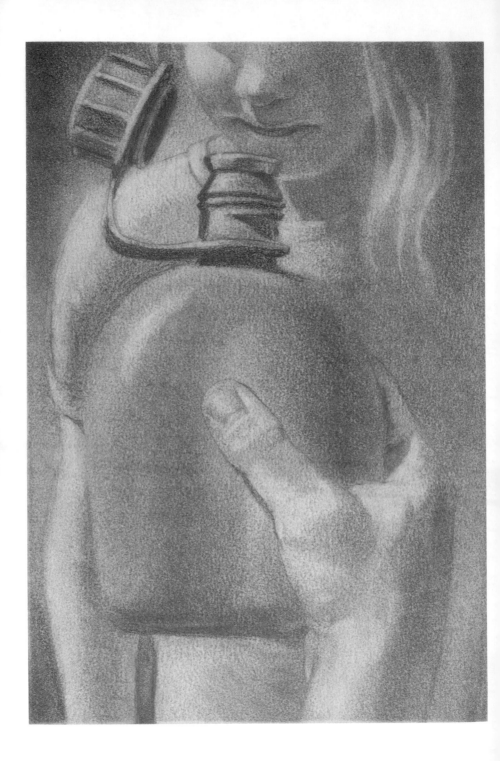

CHAPTER 10

_____

CHIILDREN: SECOND CLASS CITIZENS IN NEED OF HELP

When I can no longer bear to think of the victims of broken homes, I begin to think of the victims of intact ones. -- PETER DE VRIES

_____

Tragically, society gives lip-service to children's importance but does not allocate the resources to back up its words. Everybody has a kind word for children and no one doubts that children are the future. The problem is that many adults are more concerned with their present wants than their children's future. Society devalues everything connected with children.

Careers associated with children enjoy substantially less respect than other careers. What is considered more prestigious, being an elementary school teacher or being an engineer? A pediatrician or a surgeon? A corporate lawyer or a family lawyer? Which of these careers is given greater financial rewards? Never the ones associated with children.

Before their children were born, Ellen and Ralph made great plans for their family, the wonderful children they would have and all the advantages they wanted their children to have. Now, with an eleven year old daughter, eight year old son and six year old daughter, Ellen is busy in her career as an accountant and Ralph is climbing the corporate ladder as a vice-president of a machine tool company. Ralph and Ellen have given their children a wonderful home to live in, their own separate bedrooms, private schools, and nice clothes. Occasionally, they all go to the movies together. Ellen and Ralph don't have much spare time to actually spend with their children. Ellen and Ralph feel they are good parents and good providers but the children don't feel like their parents really care.

Ellen is excited about her new responsibilities as the head of the accounting firm's real estate department while Ralph is up for a very big promotion. The time demands of her job and Ralph's travel schedule do not allow for much time at home with the children. Ralph and Ellen are pleased to find a nanny that will be home for the kids when they come home from school and prepare dinner for them. The nanny only charges them a small percentage of their combined salaries.

The younger the child, the less respect and fewer resources society gives. It is considered progressively more prestigious to teach college than high school, high school than elementary school, elementary school than preschool. In the court system the least prestigious assignments are those in juvenile court. In personal injury awards for wrongful death, the younger the child, the smaller the award. If a child is accidentally killed because of some form of negligence, the amount of liability is actually lower when the child is younger. This is in part because younger children are viewed as more of a liability than an asset. Children, historically, have been valued by their ability to make economic contributions to the family unit. The younger the child the less valuable they were to a family. Society has progressed since the colonial period where parents reaped the fruits of a child's labor after providing initial sustenance for the child.[1] Society has failed to progress to the point where children are viewed as worthy of appropriate investment of time and money.

----

[1] For an excellent historical look at child custody issues in the United States from early colonial period forward see *From Father's Property to Children's Rights* by Mary Ann Mason.

Ralph and Ellen still have to pay for a babysitter on the weekends when they go out. They pay a neighbor $2.50 per hour to babysit. If their main babysitter is not available, however, they use a slightly younger neighbor whom they pay $1.50 per hour. They pay another neighbor $10.00 per hour to mow their lawn. Ellen and Ralph just purchased a big screen TV so their kids would have something to do at home while they are away.

Society is now reaping the disastrous harvest of its neglect of children. Society is failing to adequately invest in children and lacks any recognizable plan to deal with the problems of children. Few institutions have even bothered to identify the problems of children. The neglect of children imperils our future. Sylvia Ann Hewlett has written a shocking book entitled *When the Bough Breaks,* which graphically illustrates the alarming nature of this problem.

In society today there are unprecedented

numbers of children living in poverty, hundreds of thousands of homeless children, and a suicide rate among adolescents that has tripled since 1960. Many fathers rarely see their children after birth or divorce, and more than one fourth of all teenagers drop out of high school. With these trends and developments among young people, can anyone feel confident about the future? Is this situation the fault of the children? Are the children of today the ones responsible for this bleak picture? No. The children have not failed society, society has failed the children.

Parents are not spending time with their children and governments are too busy accommodating special interests to worry about allocating resources to children. American business has only recently started to recognize the connection between rearing children and an effective labor force. On-site child care is quickly becoming a critical component to attracting and keeping good employees.

In an increasingly global economy American business must tend to the children who will grow to fill the job roles America needs to compete effectively. An obvious starting point is for companies to help families going through divorce. By providing educational opportunities for employees on parenting, single parenting, and post-divorce parenting, companies will be contributing not only to a better adjusted present day work force but also be cultivating more enriched children who will become more effective members of the society of the future.

———————

Ralph and Ellen are concerned that their children are associating with kids from broken homes. They fear that this may be a bad influence on their children. They have not prohibited their children from playing with these kids but they have expressed their concern to their kids. Their children laughed uproariously and explained to their parents that more than half the kids at school have parents who are divorced.

———————

When a couple divorces it is rarely to promote the best interests of the children. As a result, a child's feelings and emotional well-being are not usually given top priority. When custody is decided it is usually based on how it will affect the parents, not its effect on the children. Family law matters are not given appropriate respect in our society. Courtroom time is more readily available for other trials than they are for child custody matters. Notwithstanding the unprecedented numbers of children of divorce, society still acts like an ostrich when it comes to dealing with children of divorce.

Precious few resources are allocated to the increasing number of children of divorce. It is estimated that over half the children growing up today will experience divorce or single parent families. Society neglects these children at great risk to the future of our country. While society no longer looks at children from broken homes as being tainted with some type of disease, it is still not adequately looking at the special needs of these children.

Very little is done in the area of parenting education. Since no formal education is required to be a parent and relatively few parents seek out parenting education, most children are reared by parents simply repeating the mistakes of their own parents. Parenting education is essentially viewed as a remedial step to be taken by parents who have performed so badly as to impel them into the juvenile court system. Parenting classes are not readily available nor are they recognized as generally advisable.

Parents get less guidance than individuals who care for other people's fingernails or hair. On-the-job training is the standard parenting training ground. Schools rarely offer classes in parenting or family dynamics. Old methods of dealing with the needs of children are no more suited to present day demands than a dirt road would be for major metropolitan traffic.

Children have no political clout and there is no prestige associated with children. This accounts for the dismal lack of public and private allocation of resources for children. Anything to do with children

is minimized in society.

This devaluation of children in America is like a spreading cancer. The fact that society is turning a blind eye toward the problem is a sign that it is far from coming up with a solution to a problem it refuses to acknowledge even exists. By not taking care of the children's needs now society may find that the cancer becomes inoperable in the future.

Gangs, youth crime, high school dropouts, and increasing teenage pregnancy rates are symptoms of the problem. Society must dedicate itself to a solution now. There is no time to wait. Everyone has a stake in the future of America's children. Action must be taken or the nation will suffer the consequences.

Ralph and Ellen's oldest daughter, Becky, is closely bonded with her best friend Katie. Katie's mom and dad divorced two years ago and Katie has seen very little of her dad since the divorce. Katie is very curious about Becky's parents and often discusses with Becky how much she wishes her parents were together and how much she misses her dad. Although Katie is only twelve she has already started experimenting with sex and encourages Becky to do the same.

A child growing up with only one parent is much more "at risk" than a child who enjoys two actively involved parents whether they are living together or not.

- 90% of homeless and runaway children come from single parent or sole custody situations.
- 85% of youths incarcerated in juvenile jails are from single parent or sole custody situations.
- 75% of youths at chemical abuse centers are from single parent or sole custody situations.
- 71% of all high school dropouts are from single parent or sole custody situations.
- 70% of teenage pregnancies are to children from single parent or sole custody situations.

- 63% of youth suicides are by children from single parent or sole custody situations.
- 85% of adult felonies are committed by individuals who were raised in single parent or sole custody situations.

The cost to society of neglecting these children is escalating to the point where our very society is imperiled if we continue to neglect and ignore these children. A lyric from a song by Ellen Stapenhorst entitled "If Not You" asks, "Can you stand by and do nothing because you can not do it all? If not you, if not me, who will it be?"[2] Take the challenge, take the cause and take action. Do it for the kids.

PUTTING KIDS FIRST MEANS:

- Valuing careers associated with children.
- Investing time and money in children and

---

2 Used with permission of Ellen Stapenhorst.

children's issues.

- ► Implementing parenting education programs.
- ► Taking action to improve the environment for children.

CHAPTER 11

CHIILDREN'S BILL OF RIGHTS

The best inheritance a parent can give to their children is a few minutes of their time each day. --
O.A. Batitista

The Constitution of the United States of America is synonymous with the words justice, liberty and freedom. Anything labeled "unconstitutional" is looked upon as being negative or undesirable. The main bulwark of this great document is the Bill of Rights. The Bill of Rights is so entrenched in American thought that most people, for example, recognize freedom of speech as a key part of the First Amendment and "pleading the Fifth" is not only used in court but is an accepted response to any questions one doesn't want to answer. The Bill of Rights is the great American contribution to the world human rights movement.

Despite this, children have been overlooked by the same society that so prides itself on individual rights. For example, far more rights are enjoyed by a criminal charged with a violent felony than a small child enjoys. Focusing on what inalienable rights children in America ought to enjoy will promote the types of changes that will benefit all. The following Children's Bill of Rights, if spiritually adopted by society on behalf of children, will reduce the erosion of positive family values. During a divorce, the "rights" become "requirements" for parents willing to put their kids first.

CHILDREN'S BILL OF RIGHTS

ALL CHILDREN SHALL ENJOY THE FOLLOWING INALIENABLE RIGHTS:

1. The right to be treated as important human beings, with unique feelings, ideas and desires and not as a source of argument between parents.

2. The right to a sense of security and belonging derived from a loving and nurturing environment which shelters them from harm.

3. The right to a continuing relationship with both parents and the freedom to receive love from and express love for both.

4. The right to "listening parents."

5. The right to express love and affection for each parent without having to stifle that love because of fear of disapproval by the other parent.

6. The right to grow and flourish in an atmosphere free of exploitation, abuse and neglect.

7. The right to know that their parents'

decision to divorce is not their responsibility and that they will still be able to live with each parent.

8. The right to continuing care and guidance from both parents where they can be educated in mind, nourished in spirit, and developed in body, in an environment of unconditional love.

9. The right to honest answers to questions about the changing family relationships.

10. The right to know and appreciate what is good in each parent without one parent degrading the other.

11. The right to have a relaxed, secure relationship with both parents without being placed in a position to manipulate one parent against the other.

12. The right to have one parent not undermine time with the other parent by suggesting tempting alternatives or by threatening to withhold

activities with the other parent as a punishment for the children's wrongdoing.

13. The right to be able to experience regular and consistent parental contact and the right to know the reason for not having regular contact.

14. The right to be a kid and to be insulated from the conflict and problems of parents.

15. The right to be taught, according to their developmental levels, to understand values, to assume responsibility for their actions, and to cope with the just consequences of their choices.

16. The right to be able to participate in their own destiny.

Ratify these rights for your children and you will give them better protection than any law could ever provide.

APPENDIX

SAMPLE CUSTODY AGREEMENT

The parties shall have joint legal and joint physical custody of the minor child.

SCHOOL YEAR SCHEDULE

During the school year each parent shall have physical custody of the child on an alternating week basis commencing Friday at 6:00 p.m. The parent having custody for a weekly period shall pick up the minor child at the other parent's residence at 6:00 p.m. on Friday. Mother's weekly period shall commence on [date] and father's weekly period shall commence on [date] and each parent's periods shall alternate accordingly.

ACTIVITIES OF CHILD

Neither parent shall enroll the child in any extracurricular activity without the prior approval of the other parent or as otherwise provided in this agreement. It is understood that an "activity" is defined as a long-term commitment such as soccer, baseball, hockey, karate, scouts, music lessons, etc., and shall not include short-term activities.

The parent who has the minor child shall be responsible for transportation to and from any activity of the child. Each party shall keep the other advised of all school events, teacher's meetings, and school or sports activities as they learn of them. Each party shall have the right and option to attend all school functions and activities of the minor child. Both parties shall have the right to contact any public or private school in order to procure any information regarding the child's scholastic performance. Each party shall immediately forward to the other copies of any report cards that they may receive pertaining to the child.

NOTICE REQUIREMENTS

Each parent shall keep the other advised at all times of his and her current residence address, telephone numbers (both home and work) and the child's school and also the location of any place where the child may be spending any extended period of time.

PARENTAL RESPONSIBILITIES

Neither parent shall use or make any disparaging or derogatory remarks about the other parent, or to the other parent in the presence of the child. Each party is prohibited from permitting any child to be in a place where any person (irrespective of relative, friend, significant other) is making disparaging or derogatory remarks about or about the other parent.

Each parent shall carefully avoid the scheduling or arranging of activities for the child which are likely to conflict with any visitation or period of custody allocated to the other parent.

HOLIDAYS AND VACATIONS

The children shall be with mother every Mother's Day, with the Father every Father's Day. From 8:00 a.m. to 8:00 p.m. Holidays with the minor child shall be alternated as follows: Mother shall have the first portion of the Christmas/Winter school vacation period from the day school is out until noon on Christmas Day in all even numbered years; and the second portion of said vacation period from noon on Christmas Day until school resumes in all odd numbered years. Father shall have the first portion of the Christmas/Winter school vacation period from the day school is out until noon on Christmas Day in all odd numbered years; and the second portion of said vacation period from noon on Christmas Day until school resumes in all even numbered years.

The Easter/Spring Vacation period with the minor child shall be split equally with the Mother having the first portion from the time school is out until Wednesday at 6:00 p.m. in all even numbered years and the second portion of said vacation period from Wednesday at 6:00 p.m. until school resumes in all odd numbered years. Father shall have the first portion from the time school is out until Wednesday at 6:00 p.m. in all odd numbered years and the second portion of said vacation period from Wednesday at 6:00 p.m. until school resumes in all even numbered years.

Thanksgiving vacation with the minor child shall be from Wednesday when school is out until return to school on Monday. Mother shall have the Thanksgiving vacation in all odd numbered years and Father shall have the Thanksgiving vacation in all even numbered years.

Each parent shall have two weeks of summer vacation time with the minor child. Each parent shall notify the other parent in writing of their summer vacation period by May 1 of each year. In the event of a conflict, the Mother's choice shall prevail in odd numbered years and the Father' choice shall prevail in even numbered years.

The holiday and vacation schedule shall take precedence over the regular custody schedule

IT IS FURTHER ORDERED AND ADJUDGED THAT THE PARENTS shall cooperate with respect to the child so as to a maximum degree, to advance the child's health, emotional and physical well being and to give and afford the child the affection of both parents, and a sense of security. Neither parent will, directly or indirectly, influence the child so as to prejudice the children against the other parent. The parents will endeavor to guide the child so as to promote the affectionate relationship between the child and the father and the child and the mother. The parties will cooperate with each other in carrying out the provisions of this Order for the child's best interests. Whenever it seems necessary to adjust or vary or increase the time allotted to either party, or to otherwise take action in regard to the child, each of the parties shall act in the best interests of the children. Neither party shall do anything which may estrange the other from the child or injure the child's opinion of the other party, or which will hamper the free and natural development of the child for the other party.

COMPLIANCE WITH AGREEMENT

A parent's failure to abide by the terms of this agreement may cause any or all of the following consequences:

1. Any such action may be declared null and void.
2. The offending parent may be held in contempt.
3. The Court may order that the offending parent be deprived of custody or visitation.
4. The non-offending parent may be awarded attorney fees and costs.
5. The offending parent being required to post a performance bond.
6. The Court may refuse to modify or enforce its orders against the non-offending parent.

MEDIATION AGREEMENT

1.   In the event that a dispute arises regarding of the child custody and visitation arrangements the parties shall first attempt to resolve the matter between themselves. In the event that they are unable to reach a resolution themselves they shall seek a mediated resolution as set forth herein prior to commencing any litigation.

2.   It is agreed that .... shall be the designated mediator to help the parties resolve any disputes. Each party shall be responsible for one-half of any mediation fees and costs except as otherwise provided herein.

3.   The mediator may assign greater than 50% of mediation fees/costs if the mediator determines that one party was taking an unreasonable or frivolous position.

4.   Either party may seek a judicial determination of any issue once it has been decided by the mediator and such party remains opposed to the mediator's decision. The party opposing the mediator's decision must file for judicial review of such decisions within thirty days of having received either oral or written notice of the mediator's decision.

5.   The parties agree that any decision of the mediator shall not be binding on a Court but shall be admissible in any judicial hearing, without foundation.

6.   In the event that the party seeking judicial review does not substantially prevail in Court, that party shall be responsible for all attorney's fees, mediation fees, and costs incurred by both parties relative to the determination of the issues

Putting Kids First   150

at bar. If the party seeking judicial review substantially prevails in Court, the award of any fees or costs shalt rest with the discretion of the Court. The Court shall decide whether a party has "substantially prevailed."

7. It is agreed that the initial term of the designated mediator, ... shall be for an unspecified length of time. However, either parent can request a different individual be designated as mediator after one year. The request to change mediators must be made in January of any calendar year or the designated mediator shall remain in that capacity until January of the next year.

8. In the event that either parent makes a timely request to change mediators, or in the event that the mediator is no longer available or willing to serve as a mediator, then the respective counsel for the parents will mutually designate a new mediator.

9. The term of any new mediator shall always be subject to renewal during January of each year. However, the parents can mutually agree to change the mediator at any time or designate any individual they mutually desire to serve as mediator.

AGREED:

Dated:_____ _____

Dated:_____ _____

Note

I welcome your comments, questions or suggestions concerning the issues presented in this book. You may write me directly at:

Michael L. Oddenino
ODDENINO & GAULE
444 East Huntington Drive
Suite 325
Arcadia, California   91006

For further information on the various topics discussed please contact the *Children's Rights Council* at 1-800-787-KIDS or write to:

CHILDREN'S RIGHTS COUNCIL
220 Eye Street, N.E.
Washington, D.C.   20002-4362